D1441591

THE TIDE POOL

Heather and Steven have found a new friend at the beach. While they focus their new cameras on the sea lion, several other animals that inhabit the tide pool area are hiding from view. Can you find:

Another sea lion and baby seal, sandpiper (sea bird), crab, sea gull and a pelican.

The World of Nature
invisibles

Larry Evans

Published by Troubador Press, a subsidiary of Price Stern Sloan, Inc.
11150 Olympic Boulevard, Los Angeles, California 90064
ISBN:0-8431-3490-9
10 9 8 7 6 5 4 3 2 1

TROUBADOR PRESS
a subsidiary of
PRICE STERN SLOAN

THE GALAPAGOS

Just off the western coast of South America, lies the exotic island group known as the Galapagos. Charles Darwin discovered a wide variety of animals unique to the area on his famous trip aboard the *Beagle* in the 1830's. If you look carefully, you might discover:

An extinct dodo bird, penguin, flightless cormorant (sea bird), pelican and another iguaña.

☞ **Solutions are on Pages 38 and 39.** ☜

THE CORAL REEF

Near the coastline of tropical islands and just below the ocean's surface, lie magical coral beds that support a rich variety of sea life. A whale drifts overhead, while a shark eyes the activity below. Hiding from the shark you'll spy:

A dolphin, killer whale, octopus, sea horse, another whale and shark.

THE MARSH

A heron guards his territory while waiting for his dinner to pop up from under the lily pads. Several other creatures of the wetlands are hiding in the swamp. Can you uncover:

An alligator, wood duck, mallard duck, flamingo, a duck in flight and another heron.

THE GARDEN

L ook closely at your garden and you will see an astonishingly large variety of life. The spider in her web is ready for a visit from the bumble bee. See if you can first find the big bee and then find:

Two butterflys, a snail, chameleon, tarantula, two beetles, a fly, wasp and another spider.

THE CANYON

High above the cascading river, a lone hiker stops to take a rest and enjoy the spectacular wilderness view. He has been looking all day for some of the creatures that live in the canyon. Help him locate:

A sleeping fox, hawk, bird, moose, beaver and an owl.

THE WESTERN DESERT

A prospector explores the sands for traces of gold. As he leads his burro past a natural arch created by wind and rain, he seems unaware of the animals watching him. See if you can find:

A bison, bucking bronco, scorpion, prairie dog, lizard and a coyote.

THE BIRD WATCHERS

Every year, the Robbins family hikes out to the fields to study the birds. They have been searching all day and still haven't seen even one bird. Help them find and identify:

A pheasant, turkey, parrot, sea gull, woodpecker, bat, pigeon, three birds and an extinct pterodactyl.

THE TIMBERLINE

In spring, the deer climb to the high meadows to graze on new lush vegetation. The buck is wary that other creatures may be hiding nearby. See if he's right. Find:

An eagle, bobcat, bear, bear cub, mountain lion and a hunter.

THE MOUNTAIN AERIE

A bald eagle returns to her aerie without food for her hungry chick. With luck she'll find dinner by afternoon. Other high country animals are also looking for food. Can you find:

A wolf, leaping deer, mountain goat, mountain lion and her cub, an ermine, another eagle and an extinct wooly mammoth.

THE MEADOW

The bunny is safe in her burrow nestled among the wild flowers and thistle. She thinks she is all alone, but if you look really carefully, you will find:

A horse, butterfly, mouse, cow, bull and another bunny.

THE KITTENS' JOURNEY

Coco and Carl are on a kitten adventure to the edge of the woods. They are only a short distance from the farm where they live, so several of their barnyard companions are there with them. Look for:

A swan, colt, cow, bunny, chicken, toad, two pigs and the kittens' mother.

THE HOUNDS

The foothills offer wide spaces for dogs to run and hunt. The hounds are chasing a fox, so the cat in the tree feels very safe. If she looks more closely, however, she'll notice:

A bloodhound, bulldog, beagle, cocker spaniel, basset hound, pointer and a regular mutt.

THE FOXES' DEN

In the evening the fox family emerges from its forest den to hunt for food just as the hounds and other animals are going to sleep. Among the foxes' neighbors are:

A flying quail, porcupine, two geese, a wild pig and a rooster.

RAIN FOREST

Civilization is closing in on the South American rain forest. Let's be sure its life-giving vegetation and teeming animal life don't become extinct like the beasts hidden here:

A diplodocus, triceratops, iguanodon, corythosaurus (duck-billed dinosaur) and an ichthyosaur (fish-like dinosaur).

THE ASIAN JUNGLE

Deep within the dense jungle hide the last of many endangered species. The monkey hides her baby from unseen danger. Enjoy finding these rare animals:

Three tigers, two leopards and a horn-billed bird.

THE AFRICAN SAVANNAH

A family of zebras stand under a baobab tree to escape the midday sun. Two giraffes lunch upon the high leaves of the thorn trees. The African plain hosts some of the largest, most magnificent of all wild animals. Look for:

An elephant, antelope, ostrich, charging rhino, two lions and another zebra.

AUSTRALIAN OUTBACK

Kangaroos live in Australia's wild plains known as the "outback." The rainy season has created a lush landscape for the unique animals of this large continent. Can you find:

Two emus, a crocodile, koala bear with her cub, a duck-billed platypus, another kangaroo and a kiwi bird from New Zealand.

SOLUTIONS

THE GALAPAGOS

THE CORAL REEF

THE TIDE POOL

THE MARSH

THE GARDEN

THE CANYON

THE WESTERN DESERT

THE BIRD WATCHERS

THE TIMBERLINE

SOLUTIONS

THE MOUNTAIN AERIE

THE MEADOW

THE KITTEN'S JOURNEY

THE HOUNDS

THE FOXES' DEN

RAIN FOREST

THE ASIAN JUNGLE

THE AFRICAN SAVANNAH

AUSTRALIAN OUTBACK

More Larry Evans puzzle books!

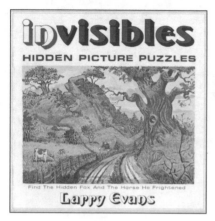

Invisibles

Invisibles two

3-Dimensional Mazes

The classic hidden picture puzzles. Their intricately detailed contests of eye, mind and wit have sold over one-half million copies. Engaging entertainment for all ages.
ISBN: 0-8431-1746-X   ISBN: 0-8431-1711-7

Amazing mazes put *you* in the puzzle with bold perspectives and daring challenges.

ISBN: 0-8431-1744-3

For over 25 years Troubador Press has been a leader in providing high quality, educational activity books to stimulate the creative best in the reader. They are available at fine book, gift, toy, museum and department stores, or may be ordered directly from the publisher.

TROUBADOR PRESS
a subsidiary of
PRICE STERN SLOAN